MAGICAL BEINGS
OF HAIDA GWAII

Illustrated by
Judy Hilgemann and Alyssa Koski

MAGICAL

Gid7ahl-Gudsllaay Lalaxaaygans
Terri-Lynn Williams-Davidson
and Sara Florence Davidson

BEINGS
OF HAIDA GWAII

Victoria | Vancouver | Calgary

Copyright © 2019 G.L. Terri-Lynn Williams-Davidson and
   Sara Florence Davidson
Illustrations copyright © 2019 Judy Hilgemann and Alyssa Koski

All rights reserved. No part of this publication may be reproduced, stored in a retrieval system, or transmitted in any form or by any means—electronic, mechanical, audio recording, or otherwise—without the written permission of the publisher or a licence from Access Copyright, Toronto, Canada.

Heritage House Publishing Company Ltd.
heritagehouse.ca

Cataloguing information available from Library and Archives Canada
ISBN 978-1-77203-296-3 (cloth)

Edited by Lara Kordic
Cover and interior book design by Setareh Ashrafolgholai
Map of Haida Gwaii by Judy Hilgemann; map icons by Alyssa Koski
   and Pauline Petit
Glossary and Pronunciation Guide compiled by *Kihlgula G̲aay.ya*,
   Severn Cullis-Suzuki, and *Jask̲waan*, Amanda Bedard
Complete image credits listed on pages 50

The interior of this book was produced on FSC®-certified, acid-free paper, processed chlorine free and printed with vegetable-based inks.

Heritage House gratefully acknowledges that the land on which we live and work is within the traditional territories of the Lkwungen (Esquimalt and Songhees), Malahat, Pacheedaht, Scia'new, T'Sou-ke, and W̱SÁNEĆ (Pauquachin, Tsartlip, Tsawout, Tseycum) Peoples.

We acknowledge the financial support of the Government of Canada through the Canada Book Fund (CBF) and the Canada Council for the Arts, and the Province of British Columbia through the British Columbia Arts Council and the Book Publishing Tax Credit.

23 22 21 20 19   1 2 3 4 5

Printed in China

*For those who came before us,
who shared another way of seeing the world.*

*For those today and in the future,
who honour and keep alive ancient teachings.*

We honour the Magical Beings of Haida Gwaii.

Introduction

Haida Gwaii: Islands of the Magical Beings

The Haida Peoples have lived in Haida Gwaii for a very long time, even before the ice age and floods made the Earth we know today. Haida Peoples have been able to live in Haida Gwaii for so long because of how the Haida view the land and the sea.

Haida Elders teach that Haida Gwaii is a magical place with Magical Beings through stories called "Raven Travelling," or *Xuuya Kaagang.ngas* in the Skidegate dialect of the Haida language. These stories tell of Raven travelling the Earth and changing it to make it fit for humans. The Haida name for Raven is *Nang Kilslas,* which means The-One-Whose-Voice-is-Obeyed. This is because Raven is powerful and can make events happen just by speaking about them.

The Inspiration for This Book

I grew up in Skidegate, Haida Gwaii. During that time, my parents, Godfrey and Mabel Williams, told me about some of the Magical Beings through Raven Travelling stories and other stories about our relatives seeing Magical Beings. My maternal great-grandmother, the late Elder and Song Keeper Susan Williams, sang songs about Magical Beings and told Raven Travelling stories in Haida. She lived until she was 109 and died when I was six years old.

I also learned about some of the Magical Beings from reading books about Haida art and culture. Later, I learned that many Haida artists, such as Charles Edenshaw and my husband, Haida Elder and Artist Robert Davidson, have always made art about Magical Beings and Crest Figures in totem poles, sculptures, tattoos, jewellery, paintings, and many other objects. I explored Magical Beings further in my discussions with Robert.

As a child and throughout my life, I tried to imagine how the Magical Beings might look. In my book and art exhibit *Out of Concealment: Female Supernatural Beings of Haida Gwaii* and my music album *Grizzly Bear Town,* I learned more about the female Magical Beings by creating images and music and writing about them.

I imagined that children today might also be curious about how the Magical Beings look. From my work with Haida musical and legal traditions, I believe it is really important for children to learn the teachings of the Magical Beings. They reinforce our shared history and connections with the land and sea and teach us how to live respectfully with the land and sea. Haida Elders teach us that everything we do affects everything else. We are all connected because, as Haida Elder *GwaaGanad*, Diane Brown, teaches, Haida Peoples were originally born of the ocean. I also firmly believe that the Magical Beings want children to know that they too are all Magical Beings with powers unique to them.

Our Shared History with Magical Beings

The entire history of the Haida Peoples is a shared history with the Magical Beings, such as *Xuuya Gaada,* White Raven, who brought Light to the World; *Jiila Kuns*, Greatest Mountain, Volcano Woman, who is the ancestress of Haida people who belong to Eagle Clans; and *SGuuluu Jaad*, Foam Woman, who is the ancestress of Haida people who belong to Raven Clans.

As time passed, the Magical Beings became part of the landscape and seascape of Haida Gwaii. They moved to live under islands, points of land, or mountains. They all have unique histories, appearances, and magical powers. Some of them helped bring human beings into existence in this world, and others helped humans survive in the early part of human history.

The Magical Beings live underneath and above Haida Gwaii. We know from the Raven Travelling stories that in their homes, they appear as humans. But when they come to visit us, they wear magical cloaks that allow them to transform. It is rare to see Magical Beings in real life. In fact, they are said to be "tickled" when people look at them.

Clans and Crests

Haida Peoples have two kinds of Clans: Ravens and Eagles. There are many different sub-clans of these two main Raven and Eagle Clans. Traditionally, people may only marry someone from the opposite Clan. Therefore, Clans guide marriage, kinship, and the ceremonial property exchanges in the Potlatch, which is the central social, political, cultural, and legal custom of the Haida Nation.

The Magical Beings also belong to either a Raven or Eagle Clan. Throughout history, there have been times when the Magical Beings (or other creatures from the land, sea, or air) interacted or helped certain people who worked hard, lived respectful lives, and had good hearts. The Magical Beings gifted those people with permission to record their shared history, to wear their images on their clothing, and to imitate them in dances. In this way, they became personal crests, or Clan crests.

Haida people wear these Crest Figures on button blankets, other regalia, tattoos, and jewellery. Wearing these Crest Figures strengthens our personal ties to our Clan, to our families, to Haida Gwaii, and to the Crest Figures and Magical Beings. Some clans have songs about Magical Beings. Haida Peoples bring Magical Beings and Crest Figures to life through regalia, songs, and dance.

The Images in This Book

This book includes ten of the many Magical Beings and Crest Figures that live in Haida Gwaii. They are shown as women for three reasons. First, to honour the central role of women in matrilineal Haida culture. Second, because many of the Magical Beings are female. And, third, because they are taken from *Out of Concealment,* which explored performance art and the identities of Indigenous women. This book contains one Crest Figure that belongs to Eagle Clans: the Frog. Because I am a Raven, the book contains more Crest Figures that belong to Raven Clans: White Raven, Mouse Woman, Lady in the Moon, Butterfly, and Rainbow. Each image shows a place in Haida Gwaii where the Magical Beings live or have appeared in the past. The map of Haida Gwaii shows the islands and some of the Magical Beings. The Magical Beings are illustrated by Alyssa Koski, of the Kainai Nation. The story of each Magical Being is told through an image of Haida Gwaii illustrated by Judy Hilgemann. Each image also contains Robert Davidson's art to help make connections to how the Magical Beings are shown in Haida art.

GID7AHL-GUDSLLAAY LALAXAAYGANS TERRI-LYNN WILLIAMS-DAVIDSON

White Raven | X̲uuya G̲aada

Before X̲uuya G̲aada
escaped from the smoke hole
to bring Light to the world,
her feathers
were white
and untouched
by the soot.

Now,
most ravens we see
are black.

But,
when X̲uuya G̲aada
returns to us,
we know
that our actions
have pushed the Earth
out of balance.

She reminds us
to be kind to the Earth
so there will be Light
for the generations
to come.

IN THE RAVEN TRAVELLING stories, *Nang Kilslas,* Raven, was born in the five-row story town of *Naayii Kun,* House Point, also known as Rose Spit.

This story is set very close to the time of the first humans on Haida Gwaii, after Raven brought Haida Gwaii into being. It takes place after Raven brought fresh water, salmon, and *Jiila Kuns,* Greatest Mountain, to the islands. It was both light and dark in the time of the Magical Beings. Raven did not like the dark, and it was said that Raven was "born for the Moon." This means that Raven was born to bring the Moon and Light to the world. In this story, Raven transformed into a hemlock needle and floated in a water hole, near the Chief's house. The Chief's daughter came to drink water, and Raven caused her to swallow the hemlock needle along with the water. Once Raven was inside the Chief's daughter as the hemlock needle, the Chief's daughter became pregnant. She gave birth to a child that was actually Raven. Raven grew quickly, like most Magical Beings that begin in human form.

The Chief was the Keeper of the Light. He kept the Light in a cedar bentwood box nested inside several other bentwood boxes. As a child, Raven constantly cried for the Light. After closing up the smoke hole at the top of the longhouse, the Chief gave in to Raven's demands and allowed the child to play with the Light. The child was happy for a while but then started crying for the smoke hole to be opened. Once it was opened, the child quickly transformed back into Raven and flew through the opening with the Light, thus bringing Light to the world.

Raven broke the Light into pieces and said to the first piece, "You shall be the Moon. Your face shall give Light in the night." Raven said to the second piece, "You shall shine in the middle of the day," and to the remaining pieces, "You shall be the Stars. When it is clear, they shall see you all during the night."

Most people think of Raven as a male Magical Being, but in some Raven Travelling stories Raven turns himself into a woman. Elder Florence Davidson also told a story in which Raven is known as "she/he." Raven can transform as needed to achieve desires and goals.

Here X̲uuya G̲aada, White Raven, is shown as a girl. X̲uuya G̲aada reminds us that we must make positive changes for the good of all beings. She returns to us when the Earth is out of balance because of our actions. We must always remember the sacrifices those who came before us have made to protect our Earth. We must also remember the sacrifices we must make, so we can share our natural wealth with those who come after us.

BEFORE RAVEN STOLE the Light and flew through the smoke hole, Raven was white. The soot of the smoke hole turned Raven black. In the picture, X̲uuya G̲aada, White Raven, is half human and half raven, with a mostly human body but also with feathers and wings. The Light is shining out from an uncovered cedar bentwood box.

Can you see the ancient design on the bentwood box and Robert's sculpture coming out of the box?

Ice Woman | *Ḵalga Jaad*

A woman of the glaciers
whose power
wove blankets of ice over the Earth.

She travelled to the islands at the edge
to catch a glimpse of Haida Gwaii.

She fell in love,
so she spared parts of the islands
from her icy embrace.

When the Earth warmed enough for human life,
she surrendered,
and travelled back, back, back,
to the place from where she came.

As she retreated,
she transformed the Earth with carved valleys,
forever leaving her mark.

Ice Woman rarely visits now,
as the Earth steadily warms.
But each time
she remembers Haida Gwaii
she sends a frosty reminder.

We honour her gift of life
by finding balance.

IN HAIDA ORAL TRADITION, *Kalga Jaad*, Ice Woman, led the Haida people from Haida Gwaii to warmer southern lands. She did this by "flying" before the coming ice, as shown here in her human form. *Kalga Jaad* is ice; ice is *Kalga Jaad*. Like any glacier, she had great physical power. As she retreated, she carved the Earth as we know it today. The power of *Kalga Jaad* was heard as she pushed trees and boulders down the watershed of *Xaana Gandlaay*, the Honna River. *Kalga Jaad* spared parts of Haida Gwaii from being covered in ice and saved some unique species from becoming extinct. Because of her, there are some species in Haida Gwaii that cannot be found anywhere else in the world.

Kalga Jaad is also a peaceful woman. According to the late Elder and Artist Charles Edenshaw, when *Kalga Jaad* was a young girl and Raven, *Nang Kilslas,* was a baby, she was one of the only Magical Beings who could quiet him. Not even his own mother could calm him. Like all Magical Beings, Raven grew quickly. But as a baby, Raven was a handful. He was demanding and cried all the time. There was never enough of anything for him, and he was always ungrateful for what he received. Only *Kalga Jaad* had enough peace to calm Raven and to help him find balance.

BECAUSE OF K̲ALGA JAAD's ability to lead people to safety, she is a role model of strength. She reminds us that we can all overcome suffering to create new life. In the picture, *Kalga Jaad* appears on Mount Moresby, the highest mountain peak in Haida Gwaii. The glacier is partially covering the mountain range. The oldest butterflies and dragonflies from Haida Gwaii appear with her.

Can you see Robert's design in the crevasses of the glacier?

Cedar Sister | *Ts'uu K'waayGa*

She is the older sister
to women
and the ally
to warriors.

She exists
in every part
of our lives.

She protects us,
provides for us,
and teaches us

to draw strength
from our community,
so that we
can always
give back.

She teaches us to listen
for the voices
of our ancestors,
so that we
remember
their teachings,

Always.

THERE IS A STRONG relationship between the cedar tree and Haida culture: our culture became what it is because of the cedar tree. In the Haida worldview, the cedar tree is every woman's older sister because she takes care of us throughout our lives. *Ts'uu K'waayGa,* Cedar Sister, is found in every part of Haida life, from the time of our birth through to every important celebration of our lives.

From the earliest times, the Haida have used cedar for homes. After the ancestress of Haida Eagle Clans, *Jiila Kuns,* Greatest Mountain, wove the first yellow cedar bark cape, Haida people have woven ceremonial regalia and baskets with cedar. Cedar is used to make planks, ropes, and tools of all kinds. It is also used in traditional games and for catching, drying, storing, carrying, and cooking food. Magical events often happen in Haida stories when people are out in the forest gathering cedar bark. In many Raven Travelling stories, warriors and Magical Beings use cedar to help humans. Some Haida Clans have cedar for crests and the right to wear cedar limbs, and there are towns and houses named after cedar.

Haida laws teach us that all beings must be respected, especially when they are giving their lives to help us. As weaver April Churchill-Davis teaches, before we take bark from a cedar tree, we must speak to the trees to learn which tree to take bark from and how much of the cedar bark we may take. We must never take too much bark from one tree.

Ts'uu K'waayGa teaches us two important laws. First, straight-grained cedar trees grow in the understorey of old-growth forests. This means we need the support of our community to grow straight and true so that we can give back to our community. Second, fallen cedar trees that return to the Earth often become nurse logs for other seedlings. This means we must seek the knowledge of our ancestors and those who have come before us.

IN THE PICTURE, Cedar Sister appears standing among her older sisters, with her arms stretched up toward the light. Her dress is simple and elegant, made of burlap with cedar bark roses coming down over her shoulder. She is also wearing a red-cedar bark headband covered with abalone shells to honour the relationship between the forests and oceans.

Can you see Robert's mask emerging from the older cedar sister?

Ts'uu K'waayGa Song

Tllgaay sda unts'idtl'lxa,
hiiGa ad yahkaa
Daa uu gina Kuuya Ga Kyahts'ii
Ad yahguudang gina
    Xaaynang.nga 'waadluxan

Rising from the land,
straight and true.
You shelter sacred,
To respect all beings.

Daa hla id sk'aadGada
kuuniisii sda hla k'aadang.nga. isda
Chiina ad taan XaaydaGa ad naawang
Ad yahguudang gina
    Xaaynang.nga 'waadluxan

You teach us,
draw from ancient wisdom
Living with salmon and
bear people,
To respect all beings.

Daanxan dang háana ga,
k'waay.yaay Ts'uu

You are so beautiful,
older Cedar Sister!

Fern Woman | *Snanjang Jaad*

Fern Woman
is the Magical Being
of new beginnings.

She is delicate in the forest,
but she is also
strong enough
to exist
in difficult places.

While protecting others,
she teaches us
to draw upon
our own strength,
which comes from
the love,
support,
and knowledge,
of family, friends, and community.

She reminds us
it is our roots
that will always
keep us strong.

S*NANJANG JAAD*, FERN WOMAN, is very important to Haida culture. She is the sister to all of the Magical Beings. In one story, *Nang Kilslas* painted his face with the design of a fern to make himself beautiful and gave Fern Woman oolichans to try to take a part of her.

In Haida stories, *Snanjang Jaad* is often with *Ḵaagan Jaad,* Mouse Woman, because she is Mouse Woman's daughter. Mouse Woman lives among the ferns in a longhouse painted with a Fern Mother design. Mouse Woman often helps and protects others. In one story, *Snanjang Jaad* protected and hid the Rusty Song Sparrow's eggs. In another story, *Snanjang Jaad* helped Marten create smoke to hide a Chief.

Traditionally, the Haida use ferns for many things: for weaving, for medicines, for steaming food in, and sometimes for eating. But we never take more than we need. The Haida respect all ferns, but the late Elder Mabel Williams taught that the ferns that grow from rocks are very special because the rocks make the ferns' medicine stronger.

IN THE PICTURE, *Snanjang Jaad* is shown unfurling in the middle of the forest among the sword ferns with a fiddlehead growing from her hand. She has a tree fern tattoo on her arm. The design comes from a coat that belonged to Susan Williams. Even though Haida Gwaii does not have tree ferns, this tattoo reminds us of our connections to all Indigenous Peoples of the Pacific, whose territory is home to the tree fern.

Can you see Robert's Mouse Woman design among the spruce trees?

Mouse Woman | _Ḵaagan Jaad_

Ḵaagan Jaad
is small enough
to hide beneath
a mushroom's cap

But she is also
powerful
beyond the limits
of our imagination

So powerful
that she does not
need to show it.

Ḵaagan Jaad teaches us
to have a kind heart,
to be generous,
and to always
trust the answers
we find
within
ourselves.

KAAGAN JAAD, MOUSE WOMAN, was once much larger than she is today. When *SGuuluu Jaad,* Foam Woman, was bringing the Haida people who belong to the Raven Clans out of the ocean, no one but Mouse Woman could approach Foam Woman. But each time *SGuuluu Jaad* blinked her eyes, *Kaagan Jaad* became smaller and smaller until she reached her present size. Mouse Woman is Fern Woman's mother. When Mouse Woman lived in Skidegate, she adopted a boy who would become a powerful Shaman known as Big Tail.

Traditionally, Haida people share stories through art as well as by telling Raven Travelling stories. According to Robert, Mouse Woman is one of the foundational elements of Haida art, appearing in almost all Haida art. Sometimes, a Haida artist creates the *Kaagan Jaad* design element on purpose, and other times *Kaagan Jaad* simply appears in their work.

In Haida stories, *Kaagan Jaad* helps humans along in their journeys and in their interactions with the Magical Beings. *Kaagan Jaad* is powerful, but she does not boast about her strength. She has a kind and generous heart, and she teaches us to follow our intuition and trust that the answers are inside us and will magically appear.

IN THE PICTURE, _Ḵaagan Jaad_ appears under a troop of mushrooms. The Haida word for mushroom is _Ḵaagan daajing,_ or mouse's hat.

Can you see Robert's Mouse Woman design above the largest mushroom on page 20?

Lady in the Moon | _Kuu.ngaay G̲a Nang Jaadas Is_

Her soul was lost to pride and anger
when her auntie's teachings
about respect for the Earth and her beings
were ignored.

The salal let her go
and she rose into the sky
up up up
to the Moon.

The salal took pity on her,
so their spirits kept her company,
connecting her
once again
to the Earth.

Her beauty can still be seen
through the moonlight
as she watches over us…

Yet she is forever alone.

But if you are quiet,
you can hear her voice
as it echoes through the moonbeams:
    "Be careful with your words,
        Be patient with your anger,
            Be present."

IN THE STORY OF *Kuu.ngaay Ga Nang Jaadas Is,* Lady in the Moon, a woman was gathering water and insulted the Moon by pointing her finger and sticking her tongue out at it. Then, as punishment, the Moon carried her away. To try to save herself, the woman grasped a salal berry bush, but the salal berry bush did not help her remain on Earth. So, to this day, she lives in the Moon. On clear nights, Haida people see her figure in the Moon, holding a basket in one hand and a salal berry branch in the other.

The Moon helps keep balance in the natural world because the Moon has both male and female energy. The Moon can help humans, such as when it made a man handsome after he had been rejected by a woman he admired. As the story of the Lady in the Moon teaches, the Moon can also remind us to behave with respect.

IN THE PICTURE, _Ḵuu.ngaay Ga Nang Jaadas Is_ holds a salal berry branch in one hand and a cedar bark basket in the other. The full moon shines over a Haida Gwaii tree line. _Ḵuu.ngaay Ga Nang Jaadas Is_ reminds us of the responsibility of every human: to be careful in how we treat others, and to respect the Earth and her beings.

Can you see Robert's Moon design that emerges from the surface of the Moon?

Frog Woman | *Hlk'yan K̲'uust'aan Jaad*

Frogs are a symbol
of our wisdom
and they remind us
to show respect.

They share their gifts
with Shamans
and bring important messages
to humans.

As we make our way
out into the world,
frogs teach us
to also look back at
the way we came.

They remind us
of the importance
of our cultural knowledge.

FROGS ARE NOT NATIVE to Haida Gwaii, but western toads are, and they are often called frogs in the Raven Travelling stories. One story tells of a man teasing a frog who turned out to be the daughter of the Chief of Frog Town. The man was taken away to Frog Town, where the other frogs asked him why he had teased the Chief's daughter. The man said it was because he wanted to marry her. The frogs allowed the marriage because the man belonged to the Frog Clan. The man and his frog-wife lived together in Frog Town. In another story, a woman married a frog and lived with him in Frog Town. She ate the food of the frogs and became green like the frogs and had children with the frog.

IN THE PICTURE, *Hlk'yan K̲'uust'aan Jaad,* Frog Woman, is shown as half-transformed between a human and a toad. She has the blotchy green-olive legs and horizontal pupils of western toads. She is basking in the pond of her natural habitat.

Can you see Robert's images of the frogs at the edge of the pond?

Swainson's Thrush Woman, "Salmon Berry Bird" | *Wiid Jaada*

Be careful
with your words,
for what you say
can change the future.

Wiid's song reminds us
of the power of our words
and assures us
the natural cycle of life
will continue.

Wiid Jaada's message is
that Indigenous cultures
will continue
to grow,
and evolve,
and to be connected
to the Earth.

WIID, SWAINSON'S THRUSH, is one of the last song birds to arrive in Haida Gwaii from the south in late May—about the time that salmon berries start to ripen. It takes three to four days for *Wiid*'s voice to warm up before it starts to sing. During that time, *Wiid* does not sing but calls. The call of the Swainson's Thrush sounds just like its Haida name, *Wiid*.

Wiid's song is magical and flutelike. One of the stories that Mabel Williams often shared is that a salmon berry ripens each time *Wiid* sings. *Wiid* breeds and spends summers on Haida Gwaii but stops singing after mating season. This is also when salmon berry season ends on Haida Gwaii.

WIID JAADA, SWAINSON'S THRUSH WOMAN, appears here in the dark, rich forests of Haida Gwaii. She is a strong Indigenous woman. She wears a vest in the earthy orange tones of ripe salmon berries. The feathers on her face and around her neck keep her connected with the gentleness of the Earth.

Can you see Robert's *Wiid* design above the salmon berry bushes? Can you see the Haida salmon berries?

Wiid Jaada Song

Dang gwa guudang?
Dang gwa guudang?
Gyuujuu hla, gam hihlda Gang!
Gina háana gii hla gyuusda
Gina háana gii hla gyuusda

Wiid k'aadang.nga giijiigid
gina sk'aadahl id tll daahlGahlda
sGaalang id tll daahlGahlda

Do you hear it?
Do you hear it?
Listen, be still!
Hear the beauty.
Hear the beauty.

Embrace *Wiid*'s wisdom,
That sound changes us.
That music changes us.

Butterfly Woman | _K̲ulG̲aay.yugung Jaad_

Butterfly-To-Be is filled with a gigantic hunger!

She is so hungry
that she eats everything that surrounds her
in her lush green world.

Then, when she is full
she hides away from the light
and escapes into her cocoon.

There,
she is protected
as she faces the unknown.

She has to fight hard on her journey.

Finally,
she comes out of her cocoon
and her transformation
is complete.

Butterfly Woman is a delicate spirit.
She is wise,
and she reminds us
to look for the good,
to be grateful for what we have,
and to always
be inspired.

O NE DAY, *NANG KILSLAS*, Raven, passed a mountain where *KulGaay.Yugung*, Butterfly, lived. Butterfly called out to Raven and offered to be his helper. At first, he refused because Raven saw that Butterfly had a big stomach and an even bigger appetite. Raven also thought Butterfly would tell lies about him. Even though Raven did not think Butterfly would make a good helper, he eventually agreed, and Butterfly became Raven's travelling companion. But Raven was right to be worried about Butterfly! When Raven was offered food for helping people, Butterfly lied about Raven and ate up the food.

As Raven's travelling companion, Butterfly sees how greedy Raven is. Butterfly does not stop Raven from being greedy, so she becomes a part of his greediness.

But Butterfly Woman is wiser than Butterfly in the Raven Travelling stories. She reminds us that sometimes we can be so greedy it feels like our greed can eat us up. The picture shows Butterfly-To-Be transformed into Butterfly Woman. Butterfly Woman was patient and waited for her transformation to happen. We can also wait and listen carefully to the voices of our hearts and our ancestors. If we are patient we might transform as well.

IN THE PICTURE, Butterfly Woman appears in the form of a Mariposa Copper butterfly. This is a kind of butterfly that can be found on Haida Gwaii. She is in a meadow of beach lupines, which grow on the sandy beaches of Haida Gwaii.

Can you see Robert's butterfly design in her wings?

Rainbow Woman | *Tawlaa Jaad*

Rainbow Woman overcomes challenges
and brings together
strength and vulnerability.

She is a being of hope
and she skillfully blends
positive and negative,
just as a Master Artist does.

Rainbows bring us light
and help us to believe
in dreams again.

Rainbows teach us to treasure
each moment of beauty.

Rainbows are the perfect invitation
to a Potlatch of laws and culture.

THE GREATEST OF THE MAGICAL BEINGS of the woods and the land is known by two names: *Kuunads*, Supernatural-One-Upon-Whom-It-Thunders, and *Didxwa Nang Kaaguns*, The-One-Travelling-Behind-Us. *Kuunads* has a town in an inlet in the Land of Souls, where the bay is covered in feathers and the songs of singing children can be heard. When we see a rainbow, it is actually the greatest of the Magical Beings, *Kuunads,* going to a Potlatch, wearing a rainbow robe to transform into a rainbow. To show respect for the greatest of the Magical Beings, we must never point at a rainbow in the sky.

IN THE PICTURE, *Tawlaa Jaad,* Rainbow Woman, wears her rainbow robe as she travels in a canoe through the feather-covered waters of the bay in the Land of Souls to the Potlatch. There are no paddlers for her canoe, as Magical Beings do not need them. She has rainbows in her eyelashes and hair, and the black marks under her eyes are the way that the Skedans Ravens show their rainbow crest.

Can you see Robert's rainbow sculpture that travels with Rainbow Woman in the Land of Souls? Can you also see *Guujaaw*'s design on the bow of the canoe?

The Critically Endangered Haida Language

Throughout Canada's colonial history, Indigenous Peoples were punished for speaking Indigenous languages. In response, the Truth and Reconciliation Commission of Canada (TRC) and the United Nations (UN) have emphasized the importance of keeping Indigenous languages alive. The UN declared 2019 to be the Year of Indigenous Languages.

The *Xaad Kil/Xaayda kil* (Haida language) was also impacted by colonialism. It is critically endangered, meaning that there are fewer than twenty fluent speakers in the whole world! New generations of language learners give hope to fluent speakers that the language is still alive and growing! For this reason, this book includes the names of the Magical Beings, and a few other words that are important to understanding the Magical Beings, in Haida. These words are described in the Glossary.

The Raven Calling Productions website contains sound files for people who are interested in learning how to say the Haida words in this book and in *Out of Concealment*: ravencallingproductions.ca/snb-glossary.

Pronunciation Guide

The Haida language is unrelated to any other language. Several of the sounds in *Xaayda kil* and *Xaad Kil* (the Skidegate and Masset dialects of Haida), are quite different than English. Here is a basic description of the sounds:

Vowels

A	as in English	*a*bove	**I**	as in English	h*i*ll
AA	as in English	f*a*ther	**II**	as in English	p*i*zza
AW	as in English	h*ow*	**U**	as in English	f*oo*t
AAY	as in English	H*ai*da	**UU**	as in English	d*u*de
EE	as in English	w*ay* (*Xaad Kil* only)	**LL**	as in English	lu*ll*

Consonants

There are well over forty consonants in Haida, and some of these don't exist in English. The best way to understand how to say something is to hear it; we have included a link to the voice recording of the words listed in the table below. A basic guide to the pronunciation of *Xaayda kil* and *Xaad Kil* consonants that are *not* found in English is given below:

NG Like the ng in "si*ng*."

J Like the j in *j*am.

HL The tongue touches the top of the mouth, and h sound pushes air to flow out the side of the mouth.

DL Voiced sound of d and l together.

TL Unvoiced sound of t and l together.

K, K', G, X These are the "back" consonants. In these cases the tongue is farther back, and the sound comes from back in the throat (an exception being the G sound in *Xaad Kil*, where the sound is so far back it is "swallowed" and there is no sound emitted).

' (OR 7) This is a glottal stop, which sounds like a break in between the English sound "Uh oh."

K', K', T', TL' When you have a ' after a consonant, this means a consonant sound with a glottal closure. You can hear a pop of air sound when the glottal closure is released.

TS' Same as in ca*ts*, with a pop of air.

'L, 'Y, 'W Glottalized consonants. When you have a ' before the consonant, the glottis has closed just before the voiced consonant is made. This is very subtle and hard for the English ear to hear.

KIHLGULA GAAY.YA, SEVERN CULLIS-SUZUKI, WITH XAAD KIL ADDITIONS BY JASKWAAN, AMANDA BEDARD

Glossary

Haida language speakers have been working hard to keep the Haida language alive, and also to ensure accurate pronunciation and spelling of Haida sounds and words. It takes significant time and effort to master *Xaad Kil/Xaayda kil* sounds, and we recognize that some of our readers will not have the background to read the language. The best practice is to *hear* how it sounds. We encourage readers to listen to the words in *Xaayda kil* and *Xaad Kil* to refine pronunciation. You can hear sound files of the words listed below here: *ravencallingproductions.ca/magical-beings-glossary*.

We also recognize that every effort to speak Haida helps! Therefore, in case you do not have web access, and to assist with reading Haida, we provide an "English approximate" pronunciation of the Haida words.

THE SKIDEGATE HAIDA IMMERSION PROGRAM Haida Words, except where noted with an *
KIHLGULA GAAY.YA, SEVERN CULLIS-SUZUKI *Xaayda kil* (Skidegate dialect) and English approximate
JASKWAAN, AMANDA BEDARD *Xaad Kil* (Massett dialect) and English approximate

XAAYDA KIL WORDS	ENGLISH APPROXIMATE	XAAD KIL WORDS	ENGLISH APPROXIMATE	TRANSLATION/ MEANING
Didxwa Nang Kaaguns	dit-hwa nuh-ng ka-g-uh-ns	Didgwaa Nang Kaagangs	dit-gwa nuh-ng ka-g-ungs	The-One-Travelling-Behind-Us
Gaajiiaawa	gah-jee-ow-wa			Haida name for Mabel Williams
Gid7ahl-Gudsllaay*	gid-uh-th-l-gud-sdlee-ya-i			Haida name for Susan Williams and Terri-Lynn Williams-Davidson
Guud san Glans	goot san glans	Guud san Glans	oat san glans	Haida name for Robert Davidson
GwaaGanad	gwa-guh-nuh-d			Haida name for Diane Brown
Hlk'yan K'uust'aan Jaad	hlk-yeah-n koos-tawn jat	Hlk'yaan K'uust'aan Jaad	hlk-yeah-n koos-tawn jad	Frog Woman *(literal: forest crab woman)*
Jiila Kuns	jee-luh koons	Jiila Kuns	jee-luh koons	Greatest Mountain
Kaagan daajing	ka-guh-n da-jing	Kagan daajanga	ka-ga-n da-jang-ah	Mushroom *(literal: mouse's hat)*

XAAYDA KIL WORDS	ENGLISH APPROXIMATE	XAAD KIL WORDS	ENGLISH APPROXIMATE	TRANSLATION/ MEANING
Kaagan Jaad	ka-guh-n jat	Kagan Jaad	ka-gah-n jad	Mouse Woman
Kalga Jaad	kuh-l-ga jat	Kalga Jaad	kuh-l-ga jad	Ice Woman
KulGaay.Yugung Jaad	kul-gai-yoo-goo-ng jat	Sdlakam Jaad	st-lah-come jad	Butterfly Woman
Kuunads	koo-nuh-ts	Kuunads	koo-nuh-ds	Supernatural-One-Upon-Whom-It-Thunders
Kuu.ngaay Ga Nang Jaadas Is	koo-ng-ai ga nung jad-uh-iss	Kungee Ga nang jaada iss	koo-ng- eh ah nung jad-uh-iss	Lady in the Moon
Lalaxaaygans	luh-luh-hai-guh-ns			Haida name for Terri-Lynn Williams-Davidson
Naayii Kun	nai-kun	Nee Kun	neigh-kun	House Point (also known as Rose Spit)
Nang Kilslas	nuh-ng kil-sl-uh-s	Nang Kilslaas	nuh-ng kil-sl-ah-s	The-One-Whose-Voice-is-Obeyed (Raven)
SGuuluu Jaad	sgoo-loo jad	SGuuluu Jaad	soo-loo jad	Foam Woman
Snanjang Jaad	sn-uh-n-juh-ng jad	Snaal Jaad	sn-all jad	Fern Woman
Tawla Jaad	taw-luh jad	Tuul Jaad	tool jad	Rainbow Woman
Ts'uu K'waayGa	choo kw-ai-guh	Ts'uu K'waayee	choo kw-ai-eh	Cedar Sister
Wiid Jaada	weet jad-uh	Wiid Jaad	weet jad	Swainson's Thrush Woman
Xaana Gandlaay	hon-nuh guh-n-dlai	Xaana Gandlee	hon-nuh guh-n-dleh	Honna River
Xaayda kil	hai-duh kil	Xaad Kil	hod kill	Haida Language (in the Skidegate dialect)
Xuuya Gaada	hoy-uh ga-duh	Yaahl Gaadas	yaath ah-das	White Raven *(literal: raven white)*
Xuuya Kaagang.ngas	hoy-uh ka-guh-ng-us	Yaahl Kaagangs	yaath ka-gah-ngs	Raven Travelling (oral narratives)

G.L. TERRI-LYNN WILLIAMS-DAVIDSON Song lyrics
THE SKIDEGATE HAIDA IMMERSION PROGRAM Haida translation

K'waay.yaay Ts'uu, Older Cedar Sister | Song Lyrics

Listen to the Xaayda kil here: ravencallingproductions.ca/cedar-sister-lyrics

XAAYDA KIL LYRICS	ENGLISH APPROXIMATE	ENGLISH TRANSLATION
Tllgaay sda unts'idtl'lxa,	tul-gai sduh oon-chid-tul-ha	Rising from the land,
hiiGa ad yahkaa	hee-ga uh-d yuh-ka	straight and true.
Daa uu gina Kuuya Ga Kyahts'ii	da oo gi-nuh ko-ya ga ki-yat-chee	You shelter sacred,
Ad yahguudang gina Xaaynang.nga 'waadluxan	uh-d yuh-goo-dung gi-nuh hai-nuh-ng-uh wa-dloo-huh-n	To respect all beings.
Da hla id sk'aadGada	duh hluh it sk-at-guh-duh	You teach us,
kuuniisii sda hla k'aadang.nga isda	koo-nee-see stuh hluh ka-duh-ng-uh iss-duh	draw from ancient wisdom
Chiina ad taan XaaydaGa ad naawang	chee-nuh uh-t tan hai-duh-ga at na-wuh-ng	Living with salmon and bear people,
Ad yahguudang gina Xaaynang.nga 'waadluxan	at yuh-goo-duh-ng gi-nuh hai-nuh-ng-uh wa-dloo-huh-n	To respect all beings.
Daanxan dang háana ga,	dan-huh-n duh-ng ho-nuh ga	You are so beautiful,
k'waay.yaay Ts'uu	kw-ai-yai choo	older Cedar Sister!

Wiid Jaada, Swainson's Thrush Woman | Song Lyrics

Listen to the Xaayda kil here: ravencallingproductions.ca/swainsons-thrush-lyrics

XAAYDA KIL LYRICS	ENGLISH APPROXIMATE	ENGLISH TRANSLATION
Dang gwa guudang?	duh-ng gwuh goo-duh-ng?	Do you hear it?
Dang gwa guudang?	duh-ng gwuh goo-duh-ng?	Do you hear it?
Gyuujuu hla, gam hihlda Gang!	jee-yoo-joo hluh, guh-m hi-hl-duh guh-ng!	Listen, be still!
Gina háana gii hla gyuusda	gi-nuh ho-na gi hluh gi-yoo-sta	Hear the beauty.
Gina háana gii hla gyuusda	gi-nuh ho-na gi hluh gi-yoo-sta	Hear the beauty.
Wiid k'aadang.nga giijiigid	weet ka-duh-ng-uh gii-juh-gid	Embrace *Wiid*'s wisdom,
gina sk'aadahl id tll daahlGahlda	gi-nuh ska-duh-hl it tul da-hl-ga-hl-uh	That sound changes us.
sGaalang id tll daahlGahlda	ga-luh-ng it tul da-hl-ga-hl-duh	That music changes us.

Further Reading: Other Children's Books That Connect to the Land

Bourdeau Waboose, Jan. *SkySisters*. Illustrated by Brian Deines. Toronto: Kids Can Press, 2002.

Campbell, Nicola. *A Day with Yayah*. Illustrated by Julie Flett. Vancouver: Tradewind Books, 2017.

Gear, Alison. *Taan's Moons: A Haida Moon Story*. Illustrated by Kiki van der Heiden with the Children of Haida Gwaii. Vancouver: McKellar & Martin, 2014.

Hainnu, Rebecca. *The Spirit of the Sea*. Illustrated by Hwei Lim. Iqaluit: Inhabit Media, 2014.

Further Reading for Parents, Educators, and Advanced Readers

Davidson, Sara Florence, and Robert Davidson. *Potlatch as Pedagogy: Learning Through Ceremony*. Winnipeg: Portage & Main Press, 2018.

Edenshaw Davidson, Florence, and Margaret B. Blackman. *During My Time: Florence Edenshaw Davidson, a Haida Woman*. Seattle: University of Washington Press, 1982.

Skidegate Haida Immersion Program. *HlGaagilda Xaayda kil K'aalang*, SHIP, *Xaayda kil* Glossary. Skidegate: Skidegate Haida Immersion Program, 2016.

The Truth and Reconciliation Commission of Canada. *Honouring the Truth, Reconciling for the Future: Summary of the Final Report of the Truth and Reconciliation Commission of Canada*. Ottawa: Truth and Reconciliation Commission of Canada, 2015.

UN General Assembly. *United Nations Declaration on the Rights of Indigenous Peoples*: resolution / adopted by the General Assembly, 2 October 2007, A/RES/61/295 ("UNDRIP").

Williams-Davidson, G.L. Terri-Lynn. *Out of Concealment: Female Supernatural Beings of Haida Gwaii*. Victoria: Heritage House Publishing, 2017.

———. *Grizzly Bear Town*. Raven Calling Productions, 2017. Compact disc.

Artwork Credits

Original illustrations of Magical Beings: Alyssa Koski
Original image backgrounds: Judy Hilgemann
Image Compositing: Pauline Petit
Art Director: Terri-Lynn Williams-Davidson

WHITE RAVEN | X̱UUYA G̱AADA
Raven Bringing Light to the World | Robert Davidson, 1984, bronze, 48 inches diameter
Vectorization of Haida art on bentwood box | Tyson G. Brown

ICE WOMAN | KALGA JAAD
Q'waaw gyaa.ang *(Wintertime)* | Robert Davidson, 2009, acrylic on canvas, 60 × 30 inches (2015 limited edition serigraph, 29 × 15.5 inches)
Vectorization of Q'waaw gyaa.ang *(Wintertime)* | Tyson G. Brown

CEDAR SISTER | TS'UU K'WAAYG̱A
Spirit of Cedar Mask | Robert Davidson, 1997, red cedar, cedar bark
Spirit of Cedar Mask Image | Kenji Nagai Photography

FERN WOMAN | SNANJANG JAAD
Kugaan Jaad Stang *(Two Mouse Women)* | Robert Davidson, 2012, red cedar, acrylic paint, 96 × 36 × 3 inches
Vectorization of Tree Fern design | Tyson G. Brown

MOUSE WOMAN | KAAGAN JAAD
The Fool in U (Mouse Woman) | Robert Davidson, 2008
Vectorization of *The Fool in U (Mouse Woman)* | Tyson G. Brown

LADY IN THE MOON | KUU.NGAAY G̱A NANG JAADAS IS
Moon | Robert Davidson, 1976, limited edition serigraph, 17 × 17 inches
Vectorization of *Moon* | Tyson G. Brown

FROG WOMAN | HLK'YAN K'UUST'AAN JAAD
Looking Back at Where We Came From | Robert Davidson, 2000, limited edition serigraph, 17 × 41.5 inches
Vectorization of *Looking Back at Where We Came From* | Tyson G. Brown

SWAINSON'S THRUSH WOMAN | WIID JAAD
Wiid | Robert Davidson, 2002, Robert Davidson, limited edition serigraph, 12.25 × 28.25 inches
Wiid | Robert Davidson, 2013, acrylic on canvas, 60 × 40 inches (excerpt of the salmon-trout head).
Vectorization of *Wiid* | Tyson G. Brown

BUTTERFLY WOMAN | KULG̱AAY.YUGUNG JAAD
Custom *Butterfly* design | Robert Davidson
Vectorization of *Butterfly* | Tyson G. Brown

RAINBOW WOMAN | TAWLAA JAAD
Rainbow | Robert Davidson, 2006, red cedar, acrylic paint, 48 × 48 × 20 inches
Rainbow image | Kenji Nagai Photography
Vectorization of Haida Art on Guujaaw's *T'aa* Canoe | Tyson G. Brown

Acknowledging Our Elders

THE SKIDEGATE HAIDA IMMERSION PROGRAM (SHIP) was founded in 1998 and is dedicated to preserving and revitalizing *HlGaagilda X̱aayda kil*, the Skidegate Haida Language. SHIP's goals are to have the Haida language once again spoken by Haida families in their households, and for future generations to speak the Skidegate Haida Language. SHIP has created and preserved a tremendous body of knowledge for present and future language learners. The average age of the SHIP Elders is eighty years, and their efforts to revitalize the Skidegate Haida Language are genuine and from the heart. Respect for Haida ancestors, the language, and its many dialects is of utmost importance to SHIP. In 2019, nine of the SHIP Elders were awarded Honourary Doctors of Laws from Vancouver Island University.

GWAAG̱ANAD, DIANE BROWN (B. 1948), is an educator, healer, and *nanaay* (grandmother). She is a language and knowledge holder of the *Ts'aahl* Eagle Clan of the Haida Nation. *Gwaag̱anad* has lived her whole life on Haida Gwaii, gathering food and learning and practising Haida medicine. She is the youngest first language speaker of *X̱aayda kil* and served her Elders and community as the first Skidegate Community Health Representative from 1970–1998 and as a founding member of the Skidegate Haida Immersion Program. She has dedicated her life to protecting her people, culture, and the Earth. Recently she starred in, and was a Haida language consultant for, the feature film *The Edge of the Knife*. Since 1986, *Gwaag̱anad* has been a member of the Traditional Circle of Indian Elders and Youth, and in 2019 she was selected as one of eight Legacy Leaders by the Spirit Aligned Leadership Program. In 2019, she was awarded an Honourary Doctor of Laws from Vancouver Island University. She has two children and four grandchildren. She lives with her soulmate, *Ganxwad,* Dullskin Brown, and together they continue to gather food, spend time with grandchildren, and speak and teach the Haida language.

GUUD SAN GLANS, ROBERT DAVIDSON (B. 1946), is a master artist who has devoted his life to the revitalization and perpetuation of Haida art, song, and dance. Robert is often credited with reconnecting community with culture through the raising of the first totem pole in nearly one hundred years in Massett, Haida Gwaii, in 1969. As he prepared for and discussed the ceremony to raise the totem pole, he recorded Elders singing Haida songs, which provided the foundation for Rainbow Creek Dancers, the dance group he co-founded with his brother in 1980. His grandparents, Florence Edenshaw Davidson and Robert Davidson Sr., were knowledgeable in Haida language, songs, culture, and botany. He learned how to carve from his father and grandfather and has received many honours for his accomplishments, including a National Aboriginal Achievement Award, the Order of Canada, the Order of BC, the Governor General's Award for Visual Arts, and six honourary degrees from universities in Canada and the US. He has hosted sixteen potlatches and feasts from 1978 to 2018. In 1996, Terri-Lynn and Robert were married in a traditional wedding ceremony that had not been performed in over one hundred years, and together they have co-hosted six potlatches and feasts. He has two children, educator Sara Florence Davidson and artist Ben Davidson, and five grandchildren: Gavin Russ, Dustin Jeanson-Davidson, and Jayde, Juno, and Jasper Davidson.

GODFREY (COLLINSON) WILLIAMS (1919–1992) was the son of the Hereditary Chief of Skidegate, Lewis Collinson. He was raised by his aunt after his mother died when he was six months old. He was selected by the village of Skidegate to go to residential school in Coqualeetza. After returning from Coqualeetza, he provided for his family through commercial fishing in the summer and fall and logging in the winter and spring. He was a beautiful singer (of contemporary western songs) and strived to achieve perfection in all that he did. He was a "silent speaker" outside of his home, but he and his wife spoke to each other in Haida. He had a deep love for Haida Gwaii.

GAAJIIAAWA, MABEL PAULINE JONES WILLIAMS (1921–2007), lived her entire life in Skidegate. She did not attend residential school, nor did any of her parents or grandparents. She was responsible for reconnecting the children in the village of Skidegate with Haida dance beginning in 1978. She made reel-to-reel recordings of her mother and grandmother. She came from a large family with twelve siblings, and did not go to school as she cared for her younger siblings. In her later years, she cared for her mother and grandmother (Susan Williams). She was a homemaker who worked hard living from the bounty and richness of the land and loved to laugh and make others laugh through her stories. She loved Haida dance, Haida botany and culture.

GID7AHL-GUDSLLAAY, SUSAN WILLIAMS (née Young née Moody), was a centenarian, who lived from 1862–1971. She was born in the village of Skedans and was a principal custodian of songs in the village of Skidegate. She was *k'uljaad*, a "Lady of High-Esteem," for she held the title of the Hereditary Chief of Skedans until others in her family could assume that title, including her brother Henry Moody, her son George Young, and her grandsons, James Wilson and Ernie Wilson. She was married to two Hereditary Chiefs, Chief Cumshewa, Samson Young, and Chief Tanu, John Williams.

FLORENCE EDENSHAW DAVIDSON (1896–1993) was born in Massett on Haida Gwaii to Charles and Isabella Edenshaw. She was an artist known for her skillful spruce root and cedar bark weaving and button blankets, which she started sewing as a young girl. She married Robert Davidson Sr. in 1911 and had thirteen children. Florence was a respected Elder in her community, and she shared her knowledge of traditional Haida life with her children and grandchildren as well as anthropologists, academics, and others interested in learning more about the Haida. In her later years, she worked hard to preserve the Haida language. She shared her life story in the collaborative autobiography *During My Time: Florence Edenshaw Davidson, a Haida Woman*, written with anthropologist Margaret B. Blackman, published in 1982.

XIIHLIIKINGANG, APRIL CHURCHILL (B. 1951), is an accomplished spruce root and cedar bark weaver from the *Gawaa Gitans Gitanee*, Eagle Clan. She comes from a family of weavers, including her *naanii Ilstayaa*, Selina Harris Adams, and her mother, *Ilskyalas*, Delores Churchill. She also comes from a family of political leaders, including her uncle, Chief *Gaalaa*, Oliver Adams (hereditary Chief and Band Councillor), and her *tsinii, Skil Gyans*, Alfred Adams, who was a central figure in the formation and operation of the Native Brotherhood of BC. She honours her ancestors' and Elders' commitment to keeping Haida art, culture, and Haida Gwaii alive, by generously and passionately sharing the knowledge and skills passed down to her. She has served as a past Vice-President of the Haida Nation, after many years of service to the Haida Nation in various capacities. In her public service, she often integrates her teachings about the spiritual responsibilities to cedar trees and eloquently teaches that a weaver is created by years of intertwined spiritual, scientific, technical, and historical knowledge. She is a proud mother of three children, a grandmother, aunt, sister, and mentor.

Acknowledgements

IN ADDITION TO the Elders recognized in the "Acknowledging Our Elders" section, there are many whose knowledge is contained in *Out of Concealment,* upon which this book is based. We thank you all, including: Abraham, of the Tanu Ravens; Chief Charles Edenshaw, of the *Sdast'aas*; John *SGaay* of the Tanu Eagles; Isaac, of Those Born at Hiellen; Chief Skedans, Henry Moody, of the Skedans Ravens; Chief Cumshewa, Job Moody, of the Cumshewa Eagles; Phillip Kitlai'ga, of the Cod People; Chief *Nan Sdins*, Tom Price, of the *SGang Gwaay* Eagles; Richard of the West Coast Eagles; Walter, of the Rear town People; and Walter McGregor of the *Ts'aahl* Eagles. We also acknowledge Peter Hamel for sharing his knowledge about Swainson's Thrush.

Thank you to the Heritage House Publishing team, especially Lara Kordic, Leslie Kenny, and Setareh Ashrafologholai. For generously agreeing to review the manuscript, thank you *Naa-Jing-Jada* (Minnie Croft would have been so happy); *GwaaGanad* (your encouragement led to this project), and Richard Van Camp—all of your kind words are truly an honour. *Haawa* again to the Skidegate Haida Immersion Program for your translations and your loving dedication to keeping *Xaayda kil* alive. Many thanks to *Kihlgula Gaay.ya* and *Jaskwaan* for the Haida Pronunciation Guide and English approximations; you both provide such hope and inspiration for a continuing, living language.

Thank you to Judy for creating glimpses of the beauty of Haida Gwaii through your watercolour illustrations. Thank you to Alyssa for bringing alive the Magical Beings and Crest Figures. We appreciate you both being willing to explore this collaboration, approaching reconciliation through art. Thank you, as always: Robert for your artwork, Tyson for digitizing the Haida art, and Pauline for seamlessly integrating all of the artists' work. We're so grateful for your beautiful art gracing this book.

TERRI-LYNN would like to thank Robert Davidson, Linda and Stephen Tollas, Elizabeth and Jasmine Bulbrook, Lara Kordic, Sharon Belanger,

Sara, Ben, Tawni, Jayde, and Juno Davidson for your creative input. *Haawa,* Robert, Linda, and *GwaaGanad* for your support and love! She also thanks Sara for agreeing to undertake this project—Sara is a gifted writer and educator, and her knowledge and expertise in Indigenous literacy transformed *Out of Concealment* into *Magical Beings.*

SARA would like to thank Angus for his ongoing support throughout all of her projects. She would also like to say *haw'aa* to Terri-Lynn for all that she does to renew our connections to our songs, culture, and history; protect lands and oceans; and ensure there is a Haida legacy for future generations.

GID7AHL-GUDSLLAAY LALAXAAYGANS TERRI-LYNN WILLIAMS-DAVIDSON is a multi-award winning Haida musician, an artist, and a lawyer, well known for her work in Indigenous-environmental law and as a keeper of traditions. She is the author of *Out of Concealment: Female Supernatural Beings of Haida Gwaii*. Born and raised in Haida Gwaii, Terri-Lynn has dedicated herself to the continuation of Haida culture. On the front lines of Indigenous Rights, she strives to open new vistas to her audiences—rooted in Indigenous worldviews, Haida language and laws, music, and oral traditions—and branches out to explore their relevance to contemporary society. *ravencallingproductions.ca*

SARA FLORENCE DAVIDSON, SGAAN JAADGU SAN GLANS, is a Haida/Settler educator and an Assistant Professor in the Teacher Education Department at the University of the Fraser Valley, where she teaches Indigenous education and English Language Arts methods. She is the co-author, with her father, Robert Davidson, of *Potlatch as Pedagogy: Learning through Ceremony*. When she is not teaching or writing, she loves walking with her dog, reading books, drinking tea, and knitting. *saraflorence.ca*

JUDY HILGEMANN grew up surrounded by art supplies and rain gear on the northwest tip of Vancouver Island. Her formal studies included graphic design and a teaching degree, with as much fine art as could possibly be woven in. In 1997, Judy and her family moved to the village of *Daajing Giids*/Queen Charlotte, Haida Gwaii, and have called it home ever since. Judy's work ranges from loose watercolour studies painted in nature to large detailed acrylic paintings to encaustic images of birds and wildlife. One of Judy's childhood dreams was to illustrate children's books, so she is thrilled to be a contributor in this latest book creation about the Magical Beings of Haida Gwaii. *judyhilgemann.com*

ALYSSA KOSKI is an illustrator, animator, and entrepreneur specializing in whimsical and narrative-based illustration, following the themes of adventure, magic, and belief in the impossible. Her work is upbeat and carefree in nature, and supports issues that are important to her, including self-confidence, respect for the environment, and the power of imagination. A member of the Kainai Nation, Alyssa is a graduate of the Alberta College of Art and Design, with a major in Character Design. She is the recipient of the Janet Mitchell Award, the Harley Brown Artistic Endowment, and the 2017 *Applied Arts Magazine* design award. She lives in Calgary, Alberta. *alyssakoski.com*